LOL
FISHING

———— • ————

by

Jack Kreismer

RED-LETTER PRESS, INC.
Saddle River, New Jersey

LOL FISHING

Revised and Updated 2012
COPYRIGHT ©2011 Red-Letter Press, Inc.
ISBN-13: 978-1-60387-004-7
ISBN-10: 1-60387-004-0

Red-Letter Press, Inc.
P.O. Box 393
Saddle River, NJ 07458

www.Red-LetterPress.com

ACKNOWLEDGMENTS

EDITORIAL:
Jeff Kreismer

•

BOOK DESIGN & TYPOGRAPHY:
Matt Taets

•

COVER & CONTENT ART:
Andrew Towl

•

PROJECT DEVELOPMENT:
Cliff Behum
Kobus Reyneke
Lori Walsh

Finally, this is to acknowledge that there will be no introduction since we are of the mindset that no one reads them, anyway. At the same time, in keeping with comedy legend Milton Berle's sentiments- "Laughter is an instant vacation"- we wish you a boatload of mini-trips with this LOL book.

–Jack Kreismer, Publisher

A fisherman who frequented a certain dockside bar had a drink named after him. It was called the "Lilac Crazy" because whenever he came in, that's exactly what he did.

Harriet's husband Herb, an avid fisherman, died suddenly one day. When she went to take care of the funeral arrangements, the local undertaker asked her how she wanted the obituary to read.

Harriet asked, "What's the cost?"

"A dollar per word," replied the undertaker.

"Okay," Harriet said. "I want it to read 'Herb is Dead'."

The undertaker responded, "I'm sorry. It's a six word minimum."

Harriet thought for a second and then said, "Okay, let's have the obituary say 'Herb is Dead, Boat for Sale'."

Supreme Court Justice Elena Kagan was invited on a fishing trip by a male friend. When they arrived at the lake, the friend suggested they rent a rowboat. "No, let's just use our wading boots and cast from the shore," said Kagan. Her friend argued about the merits of having a day in the rowboat together. At one point, Kagan responded emphatically, "No, I'm going to use my wading boots - end of discussion."

"What do you have against the rowboat?" the friend asked.

Kagan replied, "Look, I think it's long past the time to put the Roe vs. Wade argument behind us."

George and Charlie, two fishermen down in the Florida Everglades, were fishing on a small creek when out of a dense thicket of grass charged the biggest, meanest alligator anyone had ever seen.

Standing still in fear, George said to his companion, "He looks hungry. What are we going to do?"

Charlie started backing away and said, "I'm going to run for it."

"Are you crazy?" George asked in a tense whisper. "Gators have been clocked at thirty miles per hour. We'll never outrun him."

WHAT SWIMS IN THE SEA,
CARRIES A WEAPON AND
MAKES YOU AN OFFER YOU
CAN'T REFUSE?

"I don't have to outrun him," replied Charlie. "I only have to outrun you!"

A guy's terribly sick on an ocean fishing trip. Unaware of this, the captain's mate comes up to him and inquires, "We have complimentary sandwiches on board. Can I bring you one?"

The guy answers, "Naah...just throw it overboard and save me the trouble."

Herb and Clem are out at the ol' lake early in the morning when all of the sudden Clem lets go of his pole, keels over and drops to the ground. Herb fears the worst and calls 911 on his cell phone. Frantically, he says to the operator, "I'm out here fishin' with my friend. He collapsed and it doesn't look like he's breathing. I think he might be dead!"

The operator, in a soothing voice, says, "Now, calm down. Not so fast. Let's be sure he's dead."

The operator hears a shot ring out and then Herb says, "Ok, he's dead. Now what?"

A California Fisheries Department inspector boarded the ship that had just come in from a deep sea fishing trip in the Pacific. "I want to inspect your catch," he said to one angler.

"I only caught one fish...this thirteeen pound snapper. Funny thing is, when I opened him up, I noticed he'd gulped down a two pound blue. And inside that blue was this whiting."

"Give me your name and address," commanded the inspector. "That whiting is undersize."

Charlie Brown tells us that happiness is a warm puppy. To this reporter, happiness is a cold trout.

—ERIC SEVAREID

The One That Wouldn't Get Away

A Russian fisherman caught a 28-inch pike and decided to show off his trophy to his buddies. He raised the fish over his head and kissed it on the mouth.

Important safety tip to anglers everywhere: If you are going to kiss a 28-inch pike, make sure that it is dead first. In this case it wasn't, and it clamped down on the fisherman's schnozz. The fish wouldn't let go. The fisherman's screams didn't make it let go. The beating by his companions didn't make it let go. Even the fish's subsequent decapitation didn't make it let go. It took several doctors and nurses in the emergency room to finally pry the fish off. The fisherman still had his trophy, though- a mangled nose mounted in the middle of his face.

HOOK, LINE, & STINKER

Q: What do fish get if they don't like the bait that fishermen are using?

A: A re-bait

When a cop pulls a guy over for speeding, the driver claims, "Officer, I was just going with the flow of traffic."

The cop says, "Ever go fishing?"

"Yeah."

"Ever catch all the fish?"

A small town doctor was a big time fisherman. One day, while on one of his frequent fishing trips, he got a call that a woman at a nearby farm was giving birth. He rushed to her aid and delivered a healthy baby boy. The farmer had nothing to weigh the baby with, so the doctor used his fishing scales. The baby weighed 22 lbs 10 oz.

• • •

A guy walks into a seafood store with a salmon under his arm and says, "Do you sell fish cakes here?"

"No."

"Too bad," the guy says, pointing to the salmon. "It's his birthday."

Two parrots are sitting on a perch. One says to the other, "Do you smell fish?"

Dog-Fish Story

In the early 1900s, back in the days when fish could still survive in the waters of Bloomfield, New Jersey, Patrick Coffey came home with a black bass weighing over 4 pounds.

Coffey mounted the fish and placed it on a wall of the local restaurant. He then related his "fish story" to his admiring friends. He told of an uneventful day at Oakes Pond that suddenly turned exciting as he spotted movement in the water about ten feet out. He might have been getting ready to launch into a gripping account of how he bested the wily fish after a long and arduous battle, but he never got the chance. His dog, Rover, a huge Newfoundland, began howling, jumped up and charged toward the wall where the plaque with the fish was displayed. He tore the fish off the wall and proudly laid him at his master's feet.

Patrick looked at his faithful dog and smiled. He then told his friends that that was pretty much how the afternoon went as well. Rover saw the fish at the same time he did, dove in the pond and returned with the catch.

The moral of the story is that, despite all the high-tech and expensive gear anglers spend their money on, sometimes there's nothing better than a plain old four-legged fish finder.

• • •

Then there was the angler who got a hole-in-one, but went crazy trying to figure out how to mount it.

In the Jersey Pine Barrens, two fishermen were having a high old time sippin' suds and hauling the big ones in one after another. Suddenly, a game warden burst from the bushes and blew his whistle. At once, one of the fishermen dropped his rod and made a break for it. The game warden gave chase as they ran through the briars and brambles. They continued into the pine chiggers along the way. At long last, the fisherman tripped over a stump and fell to the ground, enabling the game warden to catch up.

"Have you got a fishing license, boy?" the warden breathlessly demanded.

"Certainly, sir," replied the angler. "Right here in my wallet," he said, taking out the card.

"Well, you have got to be the dumbest guy I've ever met," said the warden, shaking his head. "Don't you know you don't have to run away from me when you have a license?"

"Yes, sir," said the fisherman. "But you see, my friend back there...he doesn't have a license."

WHAT DID THE BOY OCTOPUS SAY TO THE GIRL OCTOPUS?

Reef(er) Fishing

When a 20-year-old Hong Kong man dropped his line in the water off the end of a local pier, the last thing he expected to pull up was a 33-pound bag of marijuana.

The young angler did the right thing and called the police, who surmised that smugglers had deep-sixed the pot when intercepted by a patrol boat.

Still, they took away his prized catch, which had an estimated street value of about $173,000.

Fenwick has a heart attack and dies while on a fishing trip in Montana. The other members of his fishing party are trying to figure out a sensitive way to break the news to his wife. None of them know Mrs. Fenwick, so they elect the local sheriff to inform her since they assume he's had to do that sort of thing before. The sheriff rings the Fenwicks' doorbell. When a woman answers the door, he asks, "Are you the widow Fenwick?"

She responds, "No, I'm Mrs. Fenwick."

The sheriff says, "No, you're not."

"I WANT TO HOLD YOUR HAND HAND HAND HAND HAND HAND HAND HAND."

Fisherman: Father, is it a sin to fish on Sunday?

Priest: From what I understand about the few fish you catch, it's a sin any day you fish.

Gertrude: You don't really believe your husband's story that he spent the whole day fishing, do you? Why, he didn't catch a single fish.

Gloria: That's why I believe him.

Then there was the sad, lonely fish...Seems that after the ocean fishing ship had come and gone he realized that he, in fact, was the sole survivor.

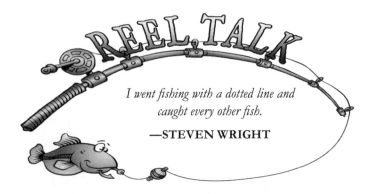

I went fishing with a dotted line and caught every other fish.

—STEVEN WRIGHT

A Texan was telling his friend about the 20 pound bass he caught. His friend asked, "Was it tough bringing him in?"

"Yeah," drawled the Texan, "but it wasn't nearly as tough as the five pound grasshopper I caught it with."

A fanatical fisherman calls his doctor and says, "Doc, you gotta help me out. It's an emergency. My baby swallowed a fish hook!"

The doctor says, "Bring him to my office. I'll meet you there."

Before the doctor can even get out the door, the phone rings again and the fisherman says, "Never mind, Doc. I found another fish hook."

HOOK, LINE, & STINKER

Q: How do you manage to keep a killer fish behind bars?

A: Strong lox

A guy goes on his annual fishing trip to Minnesota. On the boat he notices the seat next to him is empty, so he says to the guy on the other side, "Wow...to have a no-show on a big trip like this..."

The other guy says, "That's my wife's seat."

"How come she's not here?" asks the first guy. "Is she sick?"

"No. She's dead."

"Gee, I'm sorry to hear that," says the first guy. "But couldn't you find a friend or relative to take her place?"

"I'm afraid not. They're all at her funeral."

Wanted Ad

Woman who can cook, clean, wash and make sweet love.
Must have own boat.
If interested, send a photo of the boat to.....

WHAT'S THE DIFFERENCE BETWEEN A GOLFER AND A FISHERMAN?

There was a sign on a bait and tackle shop which read, "Fishing Tickle." A customer walked in, told the owner of the spelling error and then asked, "How long has that sign been like that?"

"Oh, for many years," replied the owner.

"Hasn't anyone else told you of the error?" questioned the man.

"Oh, sure. That's how I get customers."

Harry: How are you supposed to fish on a frozen lake?

Larry: Well, what I do is cut a hole in the ice and then I hold my wrist watch over it. When a fish comes up to see what time it is, that's when I net him.

• • •

Fishing for Talent

Kevin Constantine, coach of the National Hockey League's San Jose Sharks during the 1990s, made this fishy remark after his squad drafted five players from Finland: "I guess you can say we added some Finns to the Sharks."

WHEN A GOLFER LIES, HE DOESN'T HAVE TO BRING ANYTHING HOME TO PROVE IT.

Thrashing, Smashing and Trashing

At a shark fishing tournament off Destin, Fl, a captain and three anglers spent over 3 hours battling a 14-foot tiger shark that weighed well in excess of 1,000 pounds.

The first hint that this wasn't going to be an easy catch was that the specially reinforced fighting chair was torn completely off the deck by the furious fish.

Now properly warmed up, the fish proceeded to break two gimbals, a shoulder harness strap, a fighting belt and the spirits of three fishermen who did their best but were exhausted by the battle.

Finally, the well-seasoned captain took over, but the shark managed to swab the deck with him as well before breaking the line and swimming free. The damaged boat limped back to port with the fishermen all empty-handed.

At least the shark will always have the story of the four that got away.

Waldo agreed to take his little brother Wally fishing while their parents went shopping. When the parents came home, Waldo said, "I'll never take Wally fishing again. I didn't get a single bite."

"I'm sure he'll be quiet next time," said his father. "Just explain to him that noise will scare the fish and they'll swim away."

"It wasn't that," said Waldo. "He ate my bait."

St. Peter confronts a guy at the Pearly Gates. "Sorry, buddy, but you told one too many lies while you lived on earth. I can't allow you to come in here."

"Aw, St. Peter. Can't you remember when you, too, were a fisherman?"

• • •

Fish 'n Fingers

Actor James Caan, appearing on *The Tonight Show*, told host Jay Leno about the time he went fishing with a friend and caught a five-pound bass. "I took the fish home and prepared the hot oil and the bread crumbs and all of that stuff. And when I cut into this fish, my knife hit something hard. It was my thumb."

Song Title: *If Today Was a Fish, I'd Throw it Back in*

A couple of fishermen are talking. One says to the other, "I just love this sport. Man against nature. Fisherman versus fish. The fresh air. The solitude. Everything's great. And why do you fish?"

The second guy says, "Because my son's learning the trumpet."

"You know," griped Mrs. Riley to her husband, "when you come home from your little fishing trip, I ask you about your day, how they were biting, how many did you catch and so forth. But you never bother to ask me about my day. I've got shopping to do, a house to clean, four kids to watch, laundry to do... and I never get a word of interest from you."

"Sorry, dear," said Mr. Riley. "How was your day?"

"Don't ask. Just don't ask."

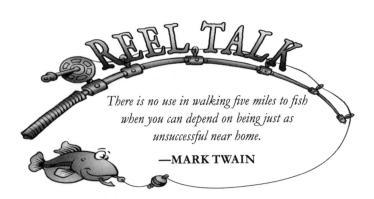

REEL TALK

There is no use in walking five miles to fish when you can depend on being just as unsuccessful near home.

—MARK TWAIN

The vessel was going down by the bow and the captain of the sinking charter boat came out on deck and asked the fishermen if anyone knew how to pray.

"Yes...I know how to pray," answered a minister.

"Good," the captain said. "Then start praying, Reverend. The rest of us will put on our life jackets...We're one short."

Smithers had a miserable time of it on the lake, not a single bite all day. On his way home, he stopped at the fish market and ordered catfish.

"Pick out four big ones and throw them at me," he told the fish monger.

"Why would you want me to throw them at you?"

"Because I want to be able to tell my wife that I caught them," replied Smithers.

"In that case, I think you should take the salmon."

"Why's that?"

"Because your wife came in and said that if you stopped by, she'd prefer salmon for dinner tonight."

Murphy was fishing in Maine even though the season was officially closed. A stranger approached him and said, "Have you caught anything?"

"Have I caught anything?" exclaimed Murphy. "I got a couple hundred pounds of the finest rock bass you ever saw iced down in my trunk."

"Do you know who I am?" asked the stranger.

"No."

"I'm the state game warden. Who are you?"

"I'm the biggest liar in the whole state."

A Whole New Meaning to "Rapping" a Fish

Remember when America declared a psychological war on Panamanian dictator Manuel Noriega and blared hard rock music around the clock to drive him from his lair? A British angler has used the music of Eminem for a similar purpose.

Mark Elmer of Birmingham reported that the fish just weren't biting in Chelmsley Wood until he happened to bring his boom box along. Contrary to the long-held belief that it is best to be quiet around fish so as not to startle them away, playing the Eminem tracks caused the fish to go into a biting frenzy. Mr. Elmer now says he catches fish by the bucketful from using his sonic secret weapon.

This Guy's Always Hooking Something on the Golf Course

While searching for a lost ball in a bunker at England's Wetherby Golf Club in 1995, Lennie Learnmouth instead raked in a 40 pound pike.

Heavy rains had caused a nearby river to flood the course, stranding the fish in the bunker until Learnmouth gaffed it with a rake, thus providing him with both the Catch and the Story of the Day at the 19th Hole.

• • •

Who Needs a Crib?

Pro golfer and avid fisherman Mike Hulbert landed a big one—8 lbs, 3 oz. to be exact. "He's just perfect for mounting," said Hulbert after taking a look at his newborn son.

HOOK, LINE, & STINKER

Q: What do sea monsters eat?

A: Fish and ships

Fish & CHIPS

After a torrential downpour, California Highway Patrol Officer
Alvin Yamaguchi was directing traffic around a flooded
intersection in the Los Angeles suburb of Irvine when he pulled a
carp over. That's not a misprint. It was a 35-pound carp that had
escaped from a nearby reservoir. Yamaguchi asked for the carp's
license and registration. When the carp refused a breathalyzer
test on the grounds that it might prove fatal, Yamaguchi nabbed
it, throwing it to drier ground where they took pictures and
prints. Well, okay, maybe not prints- but he needed the pictures,
because no one would ever believe him otherwise. Wonder if the
fish wound up in the cooler or got off the hook?

Pelican one: Pretty good fish you have there.

Pelican two: Well, it fills the bill.

**WHAT IS THE FASTEST
FISH IN THE SEA?**

Two clothing salesmen are on a fishing vacation. One says to the other, "This is really great, but I don't think it can possibly top last year's vacation."

The second clothing salesman asks, "Why's that? What did you do last year?"

"I went to Italy," responds the first clothing salesman, "and, believe it or not, I actually met the Pope."

"Wow!" exclaims the second clothing salesman. "What kind of guy is he?"

"Oh, about a 38 medium."

Dudley is applying for a job at the bait and tackle shop. The owner checks his application and exclaims, "My God! You've been fired from every place you worked! I don't think I've ever seen anything like this before!"

Dudley responds, "Yessir, I'm no quitter!"

• • •

Seen on a Tee Shirt: "To fish or not to fish ... what a stupid question!"

THE GO-CARP

A novice fisherman out on a small boat notices another guy on another small boat open up his tackle box and take out a mirror. The novice, out of curiosity, approaches the other guy and asks why he has a mirror.

"That's for catching the fish. I shine the sunlight on the water, which makes the fish come up to the top. Then I nab 'em."

"Wow! I'll give you ten bucks for that mirror," offers the novice.

"Done deal."

The novice buys the mirror, then asks the guy, "By the way, have you caught a lot of fish this week?"

"You're the eighth."

Then there was the aristocratic fish...His ancestors swam under the QE2.

*My luck! When the fish don't bite,
the mosquitoes do.*

—HENNY YOUNGMAN

A couple of anglers are boating on a lake at an Indian reservation. All of a sudden, the lake is surrounded by some natives who are more than a bit upset that these guys are fishing on their property. Off in the distance, the fishermen hear the beat of a drum. One of the guys says, "I don't like the sound of those drums."

A moment later, a distant voice yells, "He's not our regular drummer!"

Angus McCorkle, Scotland's most prominent atheist, decided that while most people were wasting their time in church on Christmas morning, it'd be a perfect time for him to go fishing. He set off in a small boat across Loch Ness until he reached the midway point and dropped his line in the water. All of a sudden, there was a great bubbling in the water. The disturbance grew and grew until McCorkle's tiny boat was lifted high into the air on the great back of the Loch Ness monster, which turned its head, bared its huge teeth and craned its long neck around to reach Angus.

Terrified, Angus cried out, "Oh, God...save me from this terrible beastie!"

From above, a deep voice boomed out, "Angus, I thought you didn't believe in Me."

Angus shouted back, "Come on and work with me a wee bit, Lord. Ten minutes ago, I didn't believe in the Loch Ness monster either!"

A newspaper ad salesman calls on Bailey, the bait and tackle shop owner. "No thanks," says Bailey. "I've been in business 27 years without spending a nickel on advertising."

"Really," says the salesman. "Say...can you tell me the name of that church across the street?"

"That's St. Mary's."

"Has it been there long?"

"More than 100 years."

"They still ring the bell, don't they?"

George is lying face down on the road with his ear to the pavement. A stranger comes up to him and says, "Hey, what are you doing?"

George says, "A green pickup truck, two fishermen in it with their poles hanging out the back... vanity license plates that say 'Gone Fishing.'"

The stranger says, "You can tell all that just from putting your ear to the ground?"

"No. I'm talking about the truck that ran me over a few minutes ago."

Two Texans went on an ice-fishing expedition in Minnesota. They gave up after only one day and returned home. When they were asked why they had come home so soon, one of them replied, "Heck, it took us six hours just to get the boat in the water!"

• • •

A Texan visits a friend in Minnesota and they go out fishing one afternoon. When his friend lands a fairly big one, the Texan says, "That's a nice fish. Can I use it for bait?"

Did you hear the one about the fishing trawler that collided with the tanker carrying red and brown paint?

The crew was marooned.

Harry: You wouldn't believe the size of the fish I caught yesterday!

Larry: How big was it?

Harry: It was so big I dislocated my shoulders describing it.

Mrs. Jones was trying to teach her second graders the importance of patience. She showed the class a picture of a boy fishing and said, "See, even things that are fun, like fishing, require patience. Why, look at that boy. He's sitting very quietly, waiting. He's very patient. Okay boys and girls, if you were going to go fishing, what is the single most important thing to have?"

A voice from the back of the class rang out, "Bait!"

• • •

Egbert was bragging to all his buddies about the humongous fish he caught.

"How big was it?" asked his friend, Willie.

"It was the biggest I've ever seen."

Willie said, "That doesn't tell me very much. Can you measure it with your hands?"

Egbert looked around the room and responded, "Yeah, but we'll have to go outside."

WHAT DID THE MUMMY
SARDINE SAY TO HER
CHILDREN WHEN THEY SAW
A SUBMARINE?

Deep in an African jungle, a guy is fishing in the river when he hears a rumbling sound behind him. He turns around and finds himself face to face with an 800-pound lion.

Immediately, the fisherman lets go of his pole and drops to his knees in desperate prayer. After a minute or so he happens to catch sight of the lion right beside him, on his knees with paws raised in supplication. Surprised, the fisherman says, "Now see here. I am on my knees praying to my Lord for deliverance. You're only a dumb animal. What could you possibly be doing?"

"Whaddaya think, Bud?" says the lion. "I'm saying grace."

Whale of a Tale

One of the inspirations for author Herman Melville's classic *Moby-Dick* was the true-life sinking of the whaling ship "Essex" by a whale in 1820. Captain George Pollard and several others aboard the ship resorted to cannibalism to survive the long ordeal.

Long after the tragedy, Pollard was approached by a relative of one of the lost crew members, who timidly asked whether the captain remembered him. "Remember him!?" exclaimed Pollard. "Hell, I ate him!"

"DON'T WORRY, IT'S ONLY A TIN OF PEOPLE."

A fishing boat goes down with only one man surviving and he's washed ashore on a remote island inhabited by cannibals. They capture him and tie him to a stake, where they proceed to nick him with their spears and drink his blood. This goes on for two weeks. The guy can't take it any longer and asks to see the chief. When the cannibal leader arrives the guy says, "Look, chief... either let me go or kill me. I'm tired of being stuck for the drinks."

Old Fisbin was leaning over the bar, crying in his beer. "My wife says if I ever go fishin' again, she's going to leave me."

"Gee, that's tough," his friend commiserated.

"Yeah," sniffed Fisbin, wiping a tear from his eye. "I'm sure going to miss her."

All men are equal before a fish.

—PRESIDENT HERBERT HOOVER

Two old fishermen, Carmine and Fenster, were out in some rough weather when Carmine suddenly lost his dentures over the side of the boat. Fenster, a sly old codger, decided to play a prank on Carmine. He removed his own false teeth, tied them on his line and made believe he had caught the missing dentures. He pulled the line in, unhooked the dentures and gave them to his friend. Carmine thanked Fenster and slipped the dentures into his mouth. After a few moments, he pulled them out and said disgustedly, "They're not mine. They don't fit!" So he threw them back in the water.

Three old geezers were sitting on a bench in New York City's Central Park. The one in the middle was reading a newspaper while the other two were pretending to fish. A policeman on the beat watched them as they baited imaginary hooks, cast their lines and reeled in their fake catches.

"Do you know these two?" the cop asked the guy reading the paper.

"Sure. They're buddies of mine."

"Well, they're disturbin' the other people. You better get them outta here!"

"Yes, officer," said the guy. With that, he furiously began rowing.

A guy went on an ocean fishing expedition and fell overboard in shark-infested waters. The guy couldn't swim and screamed for help. A lawyer who happened to be on the trip dove in to save him. All of a sudden, sharks formed a two-lane convoy and escorted the lawyer and the guy he was dragging to shore. Safely ashore, the guy thanked the lawyer profusely, but was extremely puzzled. "I don't understand it," he said. "Why did the sharks do that?"

"Simple," replied the lawyer. "Professional courtesy."

• • •

A guy rushes into a fishing supply place and hurriedly says, "I have to catch the ferry and I need some bait, quick!"

The store clerk, with a quizzical look on his face, responds, "I dunno, sir...I don't think we have any bait that a ferry would like."

You Never Know What You Might Pull Up

The word "Granny" conjures up images of lace doilies, not lace panties, but that was all Mrs. Beryl Wonson of Gloucester, Massachusetts was left with after a battle with a 755 pound tuna.

People in Gloucester take their fishing seriously, so after the genteel grandmother hooked into the huge fish, there was no going back, not even for her pants. She was buckled into a harness which started slipping down her back, pushing her trousers as it went. Naturally, she wanted to pull them back up, but her hands were busy gripping the pole. Something had to give and she decided to lose her pants rather than the fish. She kicked them free and continued the battle in her lace trimmed bikini bottoms. The men on board were embarrassed, but fishermen and gentlemen all, they averted their eyes and followed the epic battle.

When it was finally over, Mrs. Wonson got her pants back and reported that she had worked up a sweat, but the wind through her legs was very chilly. She'll always remember the incident as the day she almost caught a fish and a cold on the same outing.

Charlie's new job as a commercial fisherman promised to have him spending a lot of time at sea. Concerned for his wife's security for those times he'd be fishing the hours away, he decided to stop at a pet shop to look at watchdogs. When the pet shop owner showed him a French poodle, Charlie smirked, "C'mon, that dog couldn't hurt a flea."

"Ah, but you don't understand," said the pet shop owner. "This dog knows karate."

With that, the pet shop owner pointed to a two-by-four and commanded, "Karate the wood!" The little dog split it in half.

The pet shop owner then pointed to a thick telephone directory and instructed, "Karate the telephone book!" Again, the dog split the book in two.

Charlie was convinced. He bought the dog, brought it home and explained to his wife that he'd purchased a watchdog for her. When she saw the tiny French poodle she scoffed, "That little thing? You've got to be kidding."

Charlie remarked, "But this poodle is incredible. He's a karate expert."

"Yeah, right," Charlie's wife said. "Karate my foot."

Q: What happened when the fishing boat sank in piranha fish-infested waters?

A: It came back with a skeleton crew.

• • •

Herman: Well, the fishing wasn't so great today.

Thurman: But I thought you said you had thirty bites.

Herman: Yeah- one tiny fish and 29 mosquitoes.

IF FISH EXISTED ON LAND, WHICH COUNTRY WOULD THEY LIVE IN?

The wife is telling her friend about her recent vacation to Venice, Italy. The friend asks, "What did your husband like best about it- the art, the statues or the architecture?"

"Oh, none of those things. His favorite was being able to sit in the hotel and fish from the window."

Co-workers are talking Monday morning. One says to the other, "What did you do over the weekend?"

The other succinctly says, "Dropped hooks into the water."

The first one says, "So you went fishing, eh?"

"No, golfing."

• • •

Did you hear the one about the new horror movie where they cross a killer shark with Nessie, Scotland's most famous monster? It's called *Loch Jaws*.

When fish eat, why don't they have to wait an hour before going swimming?

FINLAND

McGee was well known for his fibs when it came to catching the big one, but one day he actually reeled in two giant flounders. He invited a few of his fishing cronies over for dinner to show off his big catches.

He had a problem, though, on how to serve the fish. He said to his wife, "If I use both fish, it'll look like I'm bragging."

Mrs. McGee suggested that he serve a piece of each flounder. "Nah," said McGee, "if I cut 'em up, they'll never believe I caught two giant flounders."

In a flash, McGee came up with an idea. That night, as his buddies were seated at the table, McGee walked into the dining room with a platter displaying one of the biggest flounders any of them had seen. Suddenly, McGee tripped and fell. At the same time, the fish platter crashed to the floor. The cunning McGee appeared to be flustered, got up and called out to his wife, "Honey, bring in the other flounder."

If you can keep your hands in your pockets and make a convincing talk about the fish that got away, you can be a successful salesman.

—MIKE RYAN

A girl went fishing for the first time with her boyfriend. As they sat in their rowboat on the lake, she asked, "How much was that red and white thing?"

"Oh, you mean the float? That's only about a nickel."

"I guess I owe you a nickel then. My float just sank."

Twin Fins

Gina and Toni Grimaldi are identical twins, even more alike than most. Fishing on a charter out of Bermuda, Toni hooked a blue marlin and fought it for 38 minutes before bringing it to gaff. Two hours later, her sister Gina hooked into a blue marlin and battled for 38 minutes before landing it. And naturally, the marlins could have been twins as well. They both weighed exactly 187 pounds.

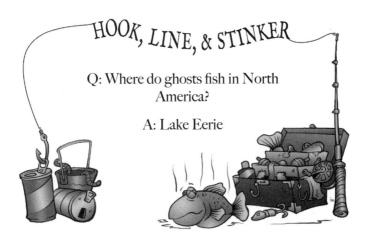

HOOK, LINE, & STINKER

Q: Where do ghosts fish in North America?

A: Lake Eerie

One day at the fishing hole, an elephant happened to notice a snapping turtle sunning itself on a rock.

Without provocation, the elephant went over to the snapper, picked it up with his trunk and threw it through the air over the trees. A fisherman with his line in the water nearby, said, "Hey, why'd you do that? That turtle was minding its own business."

"Well," replied the elephant, "I was drinking water and I happened to remember that same snapper took a chunk out of my trunk twenty years ago."

"Man! What a memory!" exclaimed the fisherman.

"All elephants have it," responded the pachyderm modestly. "It's called turtle recall."

• • •

The fisherman had a shopping cart full of angling equipment as he made his way to the cash register. Watching the cashier ring up hundreds of dollars worth of gear, he sighed, "You know, if you'd start selling fish here, you could save me a bundle of money."

Maybe you've heard about the new glass-bottomed boats. Now the fish can boast about how big the guy was they got away from.

Playing Chicken-In-The-Sea

The sea off Morro Bay, California teems with all sorts of life, and not all of it defers to fishermen. In 1998, an angler aboard a sport fishing boat hooked a salmon. It looked to be an easy catch, but suddenly, a seal grabbed the fish and wouldn't let go. The fisherman and the seal fought it out for quite some time, neither one giving ground- er, water. The battle see-sawed back and forth. The fisherman was stymied, the seal was stymied and the poor fish was totally screwed.

Finally, the captain ordered the other anglers to pull their lines from the water, and then cranked up the vessel's powerful engines to make a run directly for the seal. Unfortunately, the seal, although protected by federal law, didn't have his attorney with him at the time. He finally relinquished the fish and dove to safety as the multi-ton speeding vessel bore down on him.

It took a million dollars in equipment, violation of the Marine Mammal Protection Act and the efforts of several men, but they finally got their trophy- one badly chewed up fish.

At Sunday school, the teacher was leading a class discussion on what Noah might have done to pass time on the Ark.

"I think he went fishing," said one little girl.

The little boy sitting beside her gave her a look and piped up, "What...with only two worms?!?"

A duck walks into a convenience store and asks, "Do you sell any bait here?"

The manager says, "No, we don't carry bait."

The next day the duck walks into the store and asks, "Do you sell any bait?"

The manager says, "No, we don't have bait here."

The third day the duck walks into the store and asks, "Do you have any bait?"

The manager says, "Look! If I told you once, I told you three times- we don't have any bait here! The next time you come in here asking for bait, I'm gonna nail your webbed feet to the wall!"

The next day the duck enters the store and asks, "Do you have any nails?"

The manager says, "No. We don't sell nails here."

The duck says, "Good. Do you have any bait?"

WHAT DO YOU CALL A COUPLE THAT GOES FISHING TOGETHER?

A businesswoman vacationing in Boca Raton is strolling along the beach when she runs into a fisherman who, with his line in the water, is patiently waiting for a bite. The fisherman likes what he sees and says, "Hey, hon, would you like a little company?"

She replies, "Do you have one to sell?"

The game warden approached a boy who was fishing by the lake.

"Hey, son. Can't you read? The sign says 'No Fishing Allowed.'"

The boy whispered, "I'm fishing very quietly, sir."

Farnsworth, affectionately known as the "fishing fibber" for tales about "the big one that got away", was terribly ill. His wife, visiting him in the hospital, asked the doctor how he was doing.

The doctor responded, "I'm afraid he's lying at death's door."

"Imagine that," said the wife. "He's about to meet his maker and he's still lying."

ROD AND ANNETTE

Barney: Say, Ralph, 'member when we took that fishing trip last summer and your car broke down?

Ralph: Yeah, what a fiasco that was.

Barney: Sure was ... and remember how we wound up spending the night at that farm owned by that good-looking, wealthy widow?

Ralph: Sure do.

Barney: And remember how we slept in the guest wing of her gigantic house while she slept in her wing- and then in the morning we got our car started and headed up to the lake to go fishing?

Ralph: Yep.

Barney: Well, here it is, a year later and I got a letter from her lawyer.

Ralph: Oh, really?

Barney: Ralph, did you by any chance get up in the middle of the night and go visit her?

*Good fishing is just a matter of timing.
You have to get there yesterday.*

—MILTON BERLE

Ralph: Well, yeah.

Barney: And did you use my name instead of telling her yours?

Ralph: Sorry about that ... I did. Why do you ask?

Barney: Because she just died and left me everything.

A couple of frogs are sitting on a lily pad at the fishing hole. A fly breezes by and one of the frogs snatches it with his tongue. The other frog, looking on, says, "Time sure is fun when you're having flies."

"I have good news and bad news about your movie script," said the agent to the author of *Fish Tales*.

"What's the good news?" asked the author.

"Spielberg loved your script...He just ate it up."

"And the bad news?"

"Spielberg's my dog."

How Not to Catch a Shark

Ah, the Florida Keys. Paradise. The sun, the sand, the surf, the sharks... well, almost paradise.

Richard Burkle was fishing near the Seven Mile Bridge one day in the summer of 1961. The weather was hot and the humidity was so high that Burkle felt wetter than the fish he was going after. Totally drained from the extended battle with the big shark he had just hooked, Burkle decided to end the contest early. He would use his pistol to bring the landing to a swift conclusion.

If you ever hear anyone use the expression "It's as easy as shooting fish in a barrel," pay close attention to the "barrel" part, because otherwise, shooting fish ain't so easy. Burkle was about to pull the trigger when the shark jerked, making him slip on the wet embankment and causing him to shoot himself in the left leg.

Now that there was blood all over, the shark was even more agitated. Burkle decided that it was the better part of valor to crawl away before the creature had him stuffed and mounted.

Bleeding profusely, Burkle managed to crawl through the thick undergrowth to his car and drive himself to a police station. He was then transported on to the hospital where they took out the bullet, but couldn't restore his pride.

At least Burkle will always have the story of the one that got away- him!

Have you heard about the fishermen who complained to the United Nations that they were being harassed in international waters? The U.N. promised to mullet over.

• • •

A guy goes into a sporting goods store and says to a familiar-looking salesman, "Remember all that expensive fishing equipment you sold me a few weeks ago?"

"I certainly do."

"Remember that you told me it was well worth the expense because of all the fish I'd be catching?"

"Yep."

"Well, would you mind telling me again? I'm getting a bit discouraged."

The ladies at the coffee klatch were all admiring a huge stuffed shark which was mounted over Mabel's mantelpiece above the fireplace. Mabel grinned proudly and said, "My husband and I landed that one on a deep-sea fishing trip."

"What is it stuffed with?" asked one of the women.

"My husband."

New Meaning for the Term "Fly Fishing"

Jens Ovesen of Denmark was on a fishing vacation in Northern
Norway when he lost his footing on a steep bank, slipped and fell
into the frigid water. Swept downstream by the icy and powerful
current, Ovesen thought that he soon would be sleeping with the
fishes, but nearby, expert angler Kjell Wilhelmsen spotted his
predicament. As he went by, Wilhelmsen deftly cast his line about
30 feet and snagged the front of Ovesen's pants, reeling him in to
safety.

Ovesen celebrated his good fortune later that day by presenting
Wilhelmsen with a bottle of cognac and a new reel as a thank you.
And, since he weighed in at 246 pounds, Ovesen provided the
Norwegian with a new record catch.

An angler par excellence, Riley had the finest collection of
equipment around. When he met with an untimely death, his wife
had no idea what to do with his valued fishing possessions.

**WHAT DO YOU GET IF YOU
CROSS A WHALE WITH A
COMPUTER?**

Fortunately, she hooked up with an attorney who was able to sell the equipment for a tidy profit, thus making him the world's first reel-estate agent.

Bank customer: I need a thousand dollar loan to go on a fishing trip.

Loan officer: That might be arranged, but we need collateral. Do you own a car?

Bank customer: Oh, certainly. I have several...

Loan officer: How about a boat?

Bank customer: Sure do. As a matter of fact, I'm taking my yacht on the fishing trip.

Loan officer: And a house?

Bank customer: Oh yes. I have a townhouse and an estate in the country as well as a couple of condos in Florida.

Loan officer: Oh, come on! You must be joking!

Bank customer: Well, you started it!

A FOUR TON KNOW IT ALL

Sweet Success

Bennie Parker of Mount Pleasant, Michigan was enjoying a pleasant day of fishing with his party when he ran out of bait. Going to get more was impractical, but he found an alternative when he saw one of the kids eating Gummi worms- that popular, multi-colored squishy candy.

"Hey, it's worth a shot," Bennie thought. He put one on his hook and soon enough caught a fish. More Gummi worms went into the drink and out came more fish. Now Parker always brings a goodly supply along to use when the fish simply aren't biting anything else.

Maybe you've heard the one about the fisherman who caught a 220 pound tuna, but had to throw it back. It was a piano tuner.

There is a peculiar pleasure in catching trout in a place where nobody thinks of looking for them, and at an hour when everybody believes they cannot be caught.

—HENRY VAN DYKE

In Miami, a fisherman ran into a dockside bar and said to the bartender, "Quick, give me a drink before the fight starts."

The bartender gave him a drink and he knocked it back and ran out the door. A moment later, he ran back in and said, "Give me a drink before the fight starts."

Once again, he downed the booze and dashed out. A minute later he was back again and said, "I need a drink before the fight starts."

The bartender slammed down the bottle and snapped, "Wait a minute! Who's going to pay for all these drinks?"

The fisherman said, "Uh oh, the fight's about to start."

• • •

The answer is: Bassinet

The question: What makes fishermen happy?

HOOK, LINE, & STINKER

Q: What is a frog's favorite sport?

A: Fly fishing

Dam Nuisance

Steve Wagner of Medford, Oregon decided to get in a bit of fishing before going to work. He stopped by the Savage Rapids Dam at the Rogue River, parked his SUV and went to see how they were biting. He looked back a few seconds later to see his SUV rolling downhill. He ran in front of it, but was unable to slow it against the steep grade. He tried jumping into the moving vehicle, but only managed to get in halfway and couldn't apply the brake. Steve bailed out and ran downhill, yelling warnings to the people below. The SUV bounced off a tree and crashed into the river, taking Steve's cell phone, wallet, digital camera and fishing tackle along with it.

The truck was later recovered, but not Steve's pride. "I'll be in the book of dummies for eternity. My wife is definitely going to rescind my fishing privileges."

On the trail down to the old fishin' hole, a small boy with a fishing pole in hand ran past an old man. The old man was amused and called after the little boy, "Goin' fishing, sonny?"

The little boy called back, "Sure am."

"Got worms?" asked the old codger with a smile.

"Yep," the boy answered. "But I'm going fishin' anyway."

Sportsman #1: Have you ever hunted bear?

Sportsman #2: No, but I've gone fishing in my shorts.

A fisherman was arrested and brought to court for having caught fourteen more striped bass than the law allowed.

The judge asked, "How do you plead?"

"Guilty, your Honor," was the reply.

"That'll be 75 dollars plus costs," said the judge.

The fisherman paid the fine, then inquired of the judge, "Your Honor, if you don't mind, would it be possible to make some copies of the court record to take home to show my buddies?"

A banker went fishing with one of his customers. They were out on a boat in the river when the vessel smashed into a rock and tipped over, spilling the guys into the drink. The customer noticed the banker flailing away and said, "Say, can you float alone?"

"Oh, c'mon!" exclaimed the banker. "I'm drowning and you want to talk business!?!"

Riley and Baxter were out on the lake at the crack of dawn. They cast for trout, sat silently and kept still so they wouldn't frighten off the fish. Five hours later, Baxter shifted his feet.

"What is it with you?" snapped Riley. "Make up your mind. Did you come here to fish or to dance?"

• • •

A visitor to a local fishing spot asked one of the anglers, "Is this a good river for fish?"

"I'd say so. I can't persuade any to come out."

Two guys are out fishing for hours with nary a nibble. Finally, to break the boredom, one guy says to the other, "Say, have I ever showed you pictures of my kids?"

The other guy responds, "No, and you can't imagine how much I appreciate it."

WHAT DO YOU GIVE A SEASICK ELEPHANT?

A guy knocks on Dooley's door. When Mrs. Dooley answers it the guy says, "Hi. I'm looking for Mr. Dooley."

"He's not here," says Mrs. Dooley. "Can I help you?"

"I'm afraid not. I wanted to talk to him about our Fishing Association meeting. Do you know where I can find him?"

"Yeah...just head down to the river and look for a stick with a worm on both ends."

An avid angler on a fishing trip was at it for almost two weeks before he caught his first fish. When he got back to his hotel, he texted his wife: "I've got one. She's a real beauty...weighs seven pounds. I'll be home in a couple of days."

His wife responded with this text: "I've got one as well. She also weighs seven pounds and is a real beauty, too. Come home at once."

The answer is: The Congressional Herring

The question: What's the most powerful fish in Washington, D.C.?

LOTS OF ROOM

Brad Pitt: The Catch Who Caught Himself

Brad Pitt had to learn how to fly-cast for his role in the 1990s flick
A River Runs Through It. Practice sessions were held on various
Hollywood rooftops and were going along quite well- that is, until
Pitt hooked himself so firmly in the back of the head that the hook
had to be removed with pliers.

A lonely Bubba signed up for a dating service, explaining that
he'd had a lot of trouble finding his significant other. The reason
seemed to be his unrealistic expectations. He demanded that
the candidate be cute and short, an expert swimmer, love the
outdoors and be a fish fanatic. He was thrilled to receive a reply
the following week- until he opened it and found a picture of a
penguin.

*Fish should be cleaned immediately
after catching for best flavor and aroma.
Fishermen also smell better if they
are bathed from time to time.*
—**MILFORD S. POLTROON**

A guy saw a fisherman catch a giant trout, only to throw it back into the water. A few minutes later, he nabbed another huge trout but tossed that away, too. Then he caught a little trout, smiled and put it into his cooler for safekeeping. The guy who was watching the fisherman asked, "How come you threw away the big fish and kept the small one?"

The fisherman replied, "Small frying pan."

A couple of guys are fishing on the lake when one says to the other, "You know, I had this dream last night where I was on a fishing trip and the bass were biting like crazy. No sooner did I get my line in the water than I landed one after the other."

"Wow! I had a great dream, too," replies the second angler. "I dreamed I had a wild time with JLo and Beyonce."

"What? You dreamed you had a date with two girls and you didn't call me?"

"I did, but your roommate said you were on a fishing trip."

• • •

"My husband just left on a fishing vacation."

"How long will he be gone?"

"About 10 cases."

The owner of The Rod & Reel, a fishing gear shop, was griping to a friend about how poorly his business was doing.

"I had that problem once, too," said the friend, "but I solved the dilemma."

"How's that?"

"Simple," said the friend. "The secret is to work only half days."

"Wow! That's incredible!"

"And the best part," the friend continued, "is that it really doesn't matter which twelve hours you work."

Two young men were backpacking in the woods on a camping trip when they suddenly came upon a beautiful trout brook. There they spent the day, catching fish after fish while enjoying the fresh air and scenery. The men would be graduating from college in a few weeks and knew that they'd be going their separate ways, but made a pact that they would meet, in twenty years, at the same place and relive the experience.

Sure enough, two decades later to the day, they met and traveled to a spot near where they had been so many years before. They made their way through the heavy brush and before long came upon a brook. One of the men said to the other, "This is the place!"

The other replied, "No way."

The first man insisted, "Yes, I recognize the clover growing on the bank."

The other man responded, "You surprise me. After all these years, you should know that you can't tell a brook by its clover."

Pete takes the grieving widow of his old fishing buddy out in his bass boat to show her just where the fatal accident occurred the day before. After circling the spot for twenty minutes he looks up and says, "I know this is around the place where Al stood up and fell in. I'm sure this is where I radioed the ranger and he brought the police, but for the life of me, I can't find it."

"Find what?" sniffled Al's widow.

"The chalk outline."

The answer is Three Men and a Baby.

And the question? What do you get when four men go fishing and one comes back without having a single catch?

A guy goes to the doctor for a thorough physical. Afterwards, the doctor informs him that he needs surgery.

The guy says, "Doc, I can't have surgery now. I'm going on a big fishing trip next week. Isn't there anything you can do?"

"Well, I suppose I could touch up the x-rays."

A guy goes ice fishing in Minnesota for the first time. He's not having any luck at all, but another guy sitting close by is pulling up fish left and right. The novice ice fisherman asks the guy, "What's the trick?"

The ice fisherman mumbles, "Mmumottameepdammrmsmmrm."

"What'd you say?"

"Mmumottameepdammrmsmmrm."

"I still don't understand you."

WHAT KIND OF MONEY DO FISHERMEN MAKE?

With that, the ice fisherman opens his thermos, spits into it a couple of times and then says, "I said you've got to keep the worms warm."

The local fishing club was having its annual dinner with the usual ceremonies and trophy presentations. One of the first-timers there noticed that the chairs were spaced seven feet from each other and asked one of the club's directors how come they were so far apart.

"Oh, we always do that," said the director. "We want to make sure that the members can do full justice to their fish stories."

Egbert decided to take up fishing with the boys each Saturday. The first time he goes out, his wife prepares him a fully-packed lunch box with a hearty roast beef sandwich. When he comes home from his outing, she asks him how he liked his lunch. Egbert responds, "Not bad ... what there was of it."

The next Saturday the wife makes two sandwiches. When he comes home, once again she asks him how he liked his lunch and once again he replies, "Not bad ... what there was of it."

NET PROFITS

Exasperated, the next week his wife takes a whole loaf of Italian bread, slices it and piles on heaps and heaps of cold cuts. When Egbert comes home after fishing, he slams his lunch box on the table in disgust and says, "So I see we're back to one sandwich, eh?!?"

• • •

Whole Lotta Shark Shakin'

If you're ever face to face with a great white shark, remember to whip out your MP3 player and play some AC/DC for it- although it might be a little tricky getting those headphones on.

Scientists have discovered that the fish fancy the music of AC/DC, specifically *You Shook Me All Night Long*. In fact, it calms them down, making them more inquisitive and less aggressive. Researchers say the tune has even been known to make the huge sharks nuzzle.

A safety note for divers planning an underwater rock concert with just any old hard rock: You may attract a whole bunch of head-banging sharks, so be careful not to wind up in the "Nosh Pit".

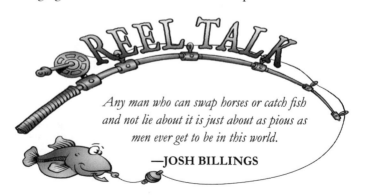

Any man who can swap horses or catch fish and not lie about it is just about as pious as men ever get to be in this world.

—JOSH BILLINGS

Fishing in the Keys

Out on the soft green banks of the Cedar River near Osage, Iowa, a man was fishing one day and hooked a big catfish. The battle went on for quite a while, but the catfish finally outsmarted him and swam away.

When the man returned to his car, he found that his keys were missing. He guessed that they had fallen out of his pocket during the epic struggle between man and fish.

The following week, he was back at the same spot and this time managed to land a fair-sized catfish. Later, while cleaning it at home, he got his car keys back- he caught the very fish that swallowed them!

The clergyman was an avid angler. During a wedding ceremony he asked the groom, "Do you promise to love, honor and cherish this woman?"

"I do," the groom replied.

The clergyman turned to the bride and said, "Okay, reel him in!"

"Just how credible is this witness?" asked the judge of the attorney who wanted to call someone to the stand.

"Your Honor, I've known him to go fishing all day and admit that he didn't have a single bite."

Gus and Pete, two old fishing buddies, were comparing their exploits, each trying to out do the other.

"Once, up in Newfoundland during a full North Atlantic gale, I caught a herring," Gus said. "And I'm tellin' you, Pete, it was the biggest herring that ever lived. It weighed at least 500 pounds!"

"That's nothing, Gus," retaliated Pete. "Down in the Keys, I pulled up my line and on the hook was a ship's lamp. On the bottom, there was the date 1392...a full century before Columbus! And get this...inside the lamp, the light was still burning!"

Gus studied his buddy's face for a few moments before cracking a smile. "Tell you what, Pete...let's compromise. I'll knock 475 pounds off the herring and you blow out the light!"

A couple of Eskimos went fishing on an extremely frigid day. They lit a fire in the bottom of their kayak to warm up, but moments later the blaze raged out of control and their boat sank. The moral of the story: You can't have your kayak and heat it, too.

• • •

A guy is eating a bald eagle and gets caught by the game warden. He's brought to trial for killing an endangered species. The judge says, "Are you aware that eating a bald eagle is a federal offense?"

The guy answers, "Yes, but I have an explanation... I got lost in the woods and didn't have anything to eat for two weeks. I saw this bald eagle swooping down for fish in the lake. I figured I might be able to steal some fish as the eagle grabbed them. Unfortunately, when I went to grab for the fish, my fist hit the eagle in the head and killed 'im. I reckoned that, since the eagle was dead, I might as well eat it since it would be a waste to just let it rot."

After a brief recess, the judge comes back with his ruling. "Due to the extreme conditions you endured, added to the fact that the bald eagle's death was accidental rather than intentional, I find you not guilty." As an aside, the judge asks the guy, "By the way, what does a bald eagle taste like?"

The guy responds, "The best way to describe it is that it tastes like a cross between an owl and an egret."

Scales of Justice or Scales of Fish?

NFL analyst Jimmy Johnson was once excused from jury duty because he was going fishing with Bill Parcells. Johnson, who had promised to take Parcells fishing, got off the hook of weighing Justice so that he could go weigh his catch.

Apparently the judge agreed that Parcells would be up the creek without a Johnson- or Evinrude- or Mercury, so Johnson was excused. Who could blame him? If you had to choose between hanging out with slimy, cold-blooded bottom feeders, wouldn't you rather it be fish than lawyers?

That Sinking Feeling

Captain Paul Campbell, of the 38 foot fishing boat Little David out of Martha's Vineyard, was trolling near Block Island when he hooked a whopper. His boat stopped its forward motion and began being towed backwards, its transom crashing squarely into the swell and throwing up huge amounts of spray. The boat shuddered and shook while the propellers spun futilely at full speed ahead. Campbell figured it had to be a whale of some sort, but it was even worse than that. Soon his stern was nearly awash and he was forced to cut loose his fishing line to save the boat.

It turned out to be a good call, for a few moments later his "catch" surfaced just astern- a US Navy submarine.

A wheeler-dealer entrepreneur was on vacation at the beach when he noticed what appeared to be a lazy fisherman sitting leisurely by the water with his pole propped up in the sand and his line cast out.

WHAT'S A DOLPHIN'S FAVORITE TV SHOW?

"Hey, bud," said the entrepreneur. "You're not going to catch any fish that way. You should be at work, anyway."

The fisherman responded, "Oh yeah? Why should I be at work?"

"Because you'll make money and then you can buy a boat which will enable you to catch more fish," said the entrepreneur.

"Why do you think that would be good for me?" questioned the fisherman.

The entrepreneur was becoming a bit irritated answering the fisherman's questions. "That would be good for you because you'd eventually be able to buy a bigger boat and hire other fishermen to work for you," he said.

"Why is that so good for me?" asked the fisherman.

Now the entrepreneur was highly agitated. "Look...you don't seem to get the point. When all is said and done, you could wind up with a whole fleet of fishing boats and amass great fortunes."

"And then what would happen?" asked the fisherman.

The entrepreneur, steaming mad, barked, "What would happen?!? You'd become filthy rich and would never have to work again! You could spend the rest of your years sitting on this beach fishing without a care in the world."

The fisherman smiled at the entrepreneur and said, "And what do you think I'm doing right now?"

WHALE OF FORTUNE

Four guys are fishing in a rowboat at the lake. A motorboat speeds by, the boat tips over and the fishermen are thrown into the water. They all swim ashore and take off their wet clothes to dry them.

Two beautiful girls pass by on jet skis. The embarrassed guys wrap their jerseys around their loins- except for one of them, who wraps his shirt around his head and face. After the girls go by, one of the fishermen turns to the guy and says, "What did you do that for?"

"Well, I don't know about you," he answers, "but the people I know usually recognize each other by their faces."

Jesus and Jake were fishing along the Galilee one day. While waiting for a bite, they struck up a conversation.

"You know, Jesus," said Jake, "you're such a great speaker with such a great message, and you do have a good following, but I think I can help you to have an even better one."

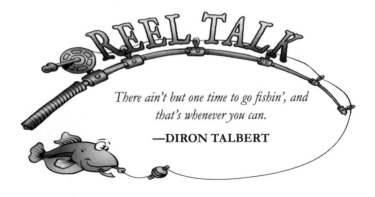

There ain't but one time to go fishin', and that's whenever you can.

—DIRON TALBERT

"How's that?" asked Jesus.

"Well, I'm a tailor, and I've noticed that you don't exactly dress to the nines. I can make you a robe that'll knock your socks off. The people will be attracted by your appearance and then by your words. The sky's the limit!"

"I don't know about that, Jake. I'm not into material things."

"Let me just give it a try," said Jake.

The two wrapped up their day fishing. A couple of weeks later, they met again. Jesus tried on the robe Jake had made for him. It was nothing short of absolutely splendid.

"Wow!" exclaimed Jake. "You look terrific, Jesus... Hey, I've got an idea! With the crowds you're going to attract, I think we should go into the clothing business. We can call ourselves 'Jesus and Jake'."

Jesus answered, "I've got a better name- Lord and Tailor."

HOOK, LINE, & STINKER

Q: What did the angler take home from the baseball game?

A: The catch of the day

Fried Fish

The wildlife got a good bit wilder the day a major pipe ruptured at the Jack Daniels distillery near Lynchburg, Tennessee, spilling almost 14,000 gallons of whiskey into Mulberry Creek.

Needless to say, the fish were sloshed to the gills for more than a mile downstream, causing a local wag to note that, for the first time in history, the fish were drunker than the fishermen!

Clem and Jethro are standing in the creek fishing on a quiet Sunday afternoon.

Clem: Did I tell you the new one I heard the other day?

Jethro: Was it funny?

Clem: Yeah.

Jethro: Then you haven't told me.

• • •

Game Warden: Hey...you need a permit to fish here!

Fishin' Fred: Why? So far I've been doing pretty good with just worms.

After the wedding and reception, the newlyweds drove off into the sunset to begin their honeymoon. They stopped at a wooded area near a lake and the husband meandered off through the trees. After about an hour, the bride decided to look for him.

Lo and behold, her hubby had borrowed some gear from an angler and was fishing beside him at the lake. "This is supposed to be our honeymoon. What's the meaning of this?" she demanded.

The husband responded, "Nagging already?"

Sherlock Holmes and Dr. Watson were on a fishing trip deep in the English countryside. They had retired for the evening and were lying there, looking up at the sky. Holmes said, "Watson, look up. What do you see?"

"Well, I see thousands of stars."

"And what does that mean to you?"

"Well, I guess it means we will have another fine day for fishing tomorrow. What does it mean to you, Mr. Holmes?"

"To me, my dear Watson, it means someone has stolen our tent."

Largemouth Bass- Wide Mouth Cans -Coincidence?

Three anglers were boating on the lake one day when Jesus walked across the water and joined them. When the flabbergasted fishermen regained their composure, one of them humbly said to Jesus, "I suffer with tremendous back pain from a schrapnel wound I got in Vietnam. Can you help me?"

"Of course," Jesus responded. With that, he touched the fellow's back and all pain was relieved.

The second guy, wearing extremely thick glasses, asked Jesus if he could do anything about his poor eyesight. Jesus nodded, removed the guy's glasses and tossed them into the water. Just like that, the man had perfect vision.

Jesus then turned to the third guy, who blurted out, "Don't touch me! I'm on disability!"

• • •

Little Johnny ran into the house, crying his eyes out. "What happened, Honey?" asked his concerned mother.

"Dad and I were fishing and he hooked a gigantic one. He fought with it for an hour, but his line broke and it got away."

WHAT KIND OF FISH DO YOU FIND IN A BIRD CAGE?

"Oh, Sweetie," his mother replied, "you're a big boy now. You shouldn't cry about something like that. You should have laughed."

"I did."

A guy goes to the doctor for a physical. Afterwards the doctor says, "I've got some good news and bad news."

The guy says, "Give me the bad news first."

The doctor says, "You've got a disease that we don't know how to treat."

"Oh my gosh! What could possibly be the good news?"

"I caught an eight pound bass yesterday."

What's the difference between a fisherman and a walrus?

One has an ugly, bewhiskered face and smells like fish... and the other one is a walrus.

A PERCH

You May Be a Fishing Widow If...

...Your bridal registry was at the bait shop.

...Your husband once presented you with a necklace made of beer tabs.

...He booked your honeymoon at the fish camp.

...You always have the uneasy feeling he's planning to leave you for Babe Winkleman.

...You find out his wedding ring often doubles as a sinker.

Q: How do fish get into business?
A: They start on a small scale.

• • •

Q: What do you call a man with a large flatfish on his head?
A: Ray

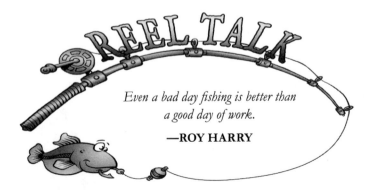

Even a bad day fishing is better than a good day of work.

—ROY HARRY

Love Bite

They say all the nuts roll downhill to Florida, and in this case it might be true. A scuba diver made a habit out of kissing nurse sharks, but one fateful day, one of the normally docile creatures took umbrage to the diver's unwanted advances. Since sharks lack arms and hands with which to slap molesting humans, they bite them in the face instead. That's exactly what happened in this particular incident, with the interspecies smooch resulting in the world's worst case of lip lock. When the shark finally let go, a swarm of snappers came in to give the hapless diver pecks on what was left of his lips.

Fortunately, there was an expert plastic surgeon at the nearby hospital who managed to reassemble most of the man's face in a long and complicated operation.

The diver's takeaway from all this? He now says that he'll never kiss another nurse shark- while it is upside down.

Tipping the Scales

Robby Rose lost his pride and his freedom after pleading guilty in 2010 to a felony charge of cheating in a Texas fishing tournament. Rose was sent to the slammer for 15 days after he admitted to stuffing a one-pound weight down the throat of a bass he'd caught. Tournament officials became just a tad suspicious when they placed the angler's fish in a tank and watched it sink to the bottom.

The President and His Pole

"When I was a small boy growing up in Kansas, a friend of mine and I went fishing, and as we sat there in the warmth of a summer afternoon on a riverbank we talked about what we wanted to do when we grew up. I told him that I wanted to be a real major-league baseball player, a genuine professional like Honus Wagner. My friend said that he'd like to be President of the United States. Neither of us got our wish."
-President Dwight D. Eisenhower

•

Calvin Coolidge, an avid if not successful angler, was once asked how many trout there were in his favorite fishing spot. The former president said that estimates ranged up to 45,000 fish. "I haven't caught them all yet," he added, "but I've intimidated them."

•

"I know the human being and the fish can co-exist peacefully."
-George W. Bush

WHAT IS THE BEST WAY TO COMMUNICATE WITH A FISH?

"The days a man spends fishing or spends hunting should not be deducted from the time that he's on earth. In other words, if I fish today, that should be added to the amount of time I get to live."
-George H.W. Bush

•

"I was president and I was fishing on the Snake River in Wyoming, and I had the secret service with me and the military aids and also the White House physician Dr. Bill Lukasz and I hung a big fish - it was a really nice fish - and I snatched the hook and the hook came loose and embedded itself in my face and there I was with this fluffy thing sticking out - you know what a fly looks like - and it wouldn't come out and I didn't know what to do. Finally, Dr. Lukasz put me on the ground and put his foot on my chest and ran a fly line through the hook and held onto it and snatched it out. So that was the biggest one I ever caught."
-Jimmy Carter

•

"All presidents go fishing, even if they have never fished before, because the American people and media have respect for privacy only on two occasions. One of them is prayer, and the other is fishing, and presidents can't pray all the time."
-Herbert Hoover

DROP IT A LINE

"There were lots of people who committed crimes during the
year (1930) who would not have done so if they had been fishing,
and I assure you that the increase in crime is due to a lack of those
qualities of mind and character which impregnate the soul of every
fisherman except those who get no bites."
-Herbert Hoover

•

'Lord, suffer me to catch a fish so large that even I in talking of it
afterward shall have no need to lie.'
-Suggested motto for President Herbert Hoover's Fishing Lodge

Fisherman: No matter where he goes, he's always dragging his
tales behind him.

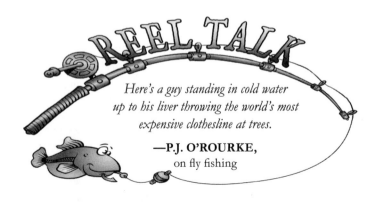

*Here's a guy standing in cold water
up to his liver throwing the world's most
expensive clothesline at trees.*

—P.J. O'ROURKE,
on fly fishing

The One That Got Away

An epic saga of sea and foam,
a man pursued his prey alone.
Time and again eluding his grip
as waves rocked and heaved his tiny ship.

The words all fishermen are doomed to say:
That was the one that got away.

Using all his experience, every trick he knew
to deny his foe to the briny blue.
Close enough at last to try a gaff,
the hook missed its mark and gouged his craft.

The words all fishermen are doomed to say:
That was the one that got away.

Neither hook nor net would land his prize
which soon was lost before his eyes.
Hope dashed in the drink, the angler was bereft
'cause now he had only a five-pack left.

The words all fishermen are doomed to say:
That was the beer that got away.

Another One That Got Away

Apparently there isn't much company when it comes to maritime
monikers in Major League Baseball. Said Atlanta Braves
broadcaster Skip Caray in the 1980s, "I wonder if (Kevin) Bass is
lonely now that Steve Trout is in the American League."

Fisherman's Horoscope

Aquarius (Jan 20-Feb 18) The Tackle Box

Born under the sign of the Water Carrier, you are still patiently
waiting for your ship to come in. Have you noticed, though, that
the tide is getting up over your hip waders?

Pisces (Feb 19-Mar 20) The Fish

It's ironic that you are a Pisces, as you have utterly no natural
ability as an angler. In fact, what you do can't properly be termed
"fishing"- it's more like you're just drowning worms.

Aries (Mar 21-Apr 19) The Net

As an Aries, your goal today should be nothing less than peace,
tranquility and oneness with the universe. If you can't swing that,
fishing and a brew sound good.

HOOK, LINE, & STINKER

Q: What fish was a famous actress?

A: Marlin Monroe

Taurus (Apr 20-May 20) The Fish Story
Born with determination and the love of the chase, you are what they call a "sport fisherman"...as opposed to one who actually catches something.

Gemini (May 21-Jun 20) The Fishing Pole
With Gemini ruling your life, you are well aware of the duality of existence. You'd do well to remember that there's a fine line between fishing and just standing on the shore looking like a dope.

Cancer (Jun 21-Jul 22) The Crab Trap
Being born under the sign of the Crab bodes ill for your domestic life. Your wife will confront you by asking which is more important—fishing or her? The real trouble will come when you respond, "Deep sea or freshwater?"

Leo (Jul 23-Aug 22) The Line
Soon, while fishing in the ocean, you'll be overcome with the certainty that all your troubles are behind you. This revelation will come as a moray eel bites through the seat of your pants.

Virgo (Aug 23-Sep 22) The Lure
You have mastered the art of thinking like a fish. In fact, you're apt to fall for anything...hook, line and sinker.

Libra (Sep 23-Oct 22) The Fish Scales
Both in your daily life and in fishing, your life has served as a beacon to others—much like a lighthouse warning people off the rocks.

Scorpio (Oct 23-Nov 21) The Bait

You are an avid fisherman who spends every spare moment and your last dollar on your passion. This explains why all other aspects of your life are pretty much "up the creek."

Sagittarius (Nov 22-Dec 21) The Hook

Born under the influence of this sign, your delusions of fishing are doomed to failure. You couldn't catch a fish if it were coated in batter and swimming in tartar sauce.

Capricorn (Dec 22-Jan 19) The Boot

The stars predict that you will soon sign a multi-million dollar endorsement contract for the world's leading rod and reel manufacturer. Now your only problem will be getting them to sign it!

Former talk show host Dick Cavett provided the punch line for this one: Speaking of an undersized fish which was caught by an angler on the polluted Hudson River, Cavett remarked, "The fish begged the man not to throw him back."

WHY DO THEY CUT THE HEADS OFF OF SARDINES?

Loony Laws of the Land- And Sea
Laughable legislation that just might still be on the books!

In Ohio, it's illegal to fish for whales on Sunday. It is also against the law at any time to get a fish drunk in the Buckeye State.

•

In Tennessee, the use of a lasso to catch a fish is strictly forbidden.

•

You are breaking the law in Chicago, Illinois if you fish in your pajamas.

•

Another Chicago law makes it illegal to fish while on a giraffe's neck. Similarly, in Idaho, you may not fish on an alligator's back.

•

In Utah, it's against the law to fish from horseback.

•

In Oregon, canned corn is not to be used as bait for fishing.

SO THEY DON'T BITE EACH OTHER IN THE CAN

No one is allowed to catch a fish with only bare hands in Kansas.

•

In California, it is a misdemeanor to shoot at any kind of game from a moving vehicle, unless the target is a whale.

•

A New Jersey statute makes it illegal for a man to knit during the fishing season.

•

In Montana, it is illegal for married women to go fishing alone on Sundays and illegal for unmarried women to fish alone, period.

•

In Kentucky, you'll be breaking the law if you fish in the Ohio River without an Indiana Fishing License.

Fishermen are born honest,
but they get over it.

—ED ZERN

A Fisherman's Wake

Angler Pete Hodge sleeps with the fishes. He wanted it that way. An avid fisherman, Pete's dying wish in 2008 was to give back to his finny friends who had brought him so much joy over the years- and also to bring them together one last time so his human friends could send as many of them as possible to the next life along with Pete.

Pete's wife had him cremated in a wicker fishing basket type of coffin, his ashes mixed with some tasty ingredients and used as ground bait. His buddies tossed the little balls of Pete-based bait into the water at Pete's favorite fishing spot and soon the fish showed up to pay their respects to their former foe. Some acted as tiny pallbearers, carrying bits of Pete away downstream, while others acted as dinner for Pete's fishing buddies.

All in all, not a bad sendoff for a fisherman who's reached the end of the line.

Forget the Shrimp- Let's Throw Another Catfish on the Barbie

David Hayes was proud to establish the North Carolina state record catch for channel catfish at 21 pounds, 1 ounce. What he was not so proud of was the fact that he did it with a Barbie fishing pole. His granddaughter had asked him to hold her pole while she took a bathroom break. That's when the catfish decided to strike, making David's greatest fishing memory one of a pink rod and red cheeks.

Fishin' Obstetrician

When most husbands get the call that their wife is about to give birth, they grab her suitcase and head for the door. When British angler Jeremy Cunningham heard his wife yelling from the bathroom, he headed for his tackle box instead.

The early morning delivery came so suddenly that by the time Jeremy got to the bathroom, the baby had been born- but his wife was in need of some medical attention. That's when Jeremy knew it was time to fish or cut bait. He dashed out and was back in a flash with the only tools he knew how to use. He clamped the umbilical cord with his new fish hook remover. When the doctor arrived, he needed more light to work by, so out came Jeremy's fishing hat with a miner's lamp on the front.

Mother and baby were just fine and, always a fisherman at heart, Jeremy was not only a proud papa, but happy he landed a whopper to boot!

HOOK, LINE, & STINKER

Q: What do Texans call sushi?

A: Bait

Where's the Partridge in a Pear Tree?

In *Jaws*, Quint said that he saw a shark eat a rocking chair once, and of course there was the famous scene where they pulled a license plate out of a shark's stomach.

Now in case you're keeping track, here is a brief list of other things found in sharks' bellies from various locales:

A Philippine shark:
7 pairs of stockings
47 buttons
3 leather belts
9 shoes
-Sounds heavily influenced by Imelda Marcos

An Adriatic shark:
A raincoat
3 overcoats
And the iconic license plate
*-Obviously a shark with a taste for tin, who also wanted
to stay warm and dry on the inside*

Mediterranean shark:
1 partially digested suit of armor with a headless man inside
*-The Continental sophistication of dining on fine canned human,
a must when they are out of season*

Thumbing for Trout

On a beautiful summer day at the Flaming Gorge Reservoir, a man was enjoying sitting on the bow of a ski boat. Suddenly, a wake from a speeding houseboat slammed into the hull and threw him over the side. He found himself under the boat trying to escape its spinning propeller. Unfortunately, his hand was sucked through the powerful prop and, besides inflicting other serious injuries, the propeller cut his thumb off.

Seventeen days later, he emerged from the hospital. His thumb did not. That was gone forever- or so he thought. About seven months later, there was a story in the paper about a fisherman at Flaming Gorge who had caught a trout with a thumb in its stomach just hours after the man's accident. The angler contacted the authorities and the thumb was given over to the coroner. Seeing the story, the injured man called to inquire as to the detached digit.

Eventually, the man was called to identify the thumb. They took it out of the cooler, presumably an ice cube tray- and pulled back

WHAT DID THE PRIEST SAY WHEN ASKED IF HE THOUGHT HE'D CATCH ANY FISH?

the sheet- or maybe it was a handkerchief. The man gasped and positively identified the well preserved thumb.

Being the thumb's next of kin, the coroner's office turned it over to the man, who now keeps it close at hand in a pickle jar.

A gorilla perched on a tree limb right next to a lake notices that just below him, a lion has cast a line and appears to have settled in for an afternoon of fishing. The gorilla decides to pull a little surprise on the king of the jungle. He leaps from the tree, lands on the lion's back and lets out a ferocious growl. He catches the lion by surprise, alright. The lion lets go of the pole and runs out from underneath the gorilla's grasp straight into the water.

Now the gorilla knows the lion is going to be enraged, so he takes off and runs into the woods. Once the lion regains his senses and realizes what's happened, he becomes hopping mad and begins to take chase.

The gorilla figures he's no match for the lion's speed, so he looks for a place to duck for cover. He spots a tent and runs inside, where he sees a hunter sitting there, reading the newspaper. When the hunter notices the gorilla, he immediately bolts from the tent.

"COD WILLING,"

The gorilla quickly takes the hunter's hat from the chair, puts it on, sits down, grabs the newspaper and covers his face as if to be reading it.

Meanwhile, the lion, in hot pursuit, comes to a screeching halt when he reaches the tent. He peers inside and sees someone reading the newspaper. "Hey, buddy," roars the lion, "Did you see anyone come running by here?"

The gorilla never looks up from behind the paper and says, "You mean the gorilla that jumped you from behind?"

The lion groans, "Oh, no. You mean to tell me it's in the paper already?"

• • •

Another Juiced Fisherman

A Ukrainian fisherman had a bright idea one day. He rigged the power from his house to long cables, which he carried down to the river and threw in the water. As he had figured, electrocuted fish floated to the surface almost immediately.

If people concentrated on the really important things in life, there'd be a shortage of fishing poles.

—DOUG LARSON

The fisherman was so excited one of his schemes finally worked, he waded into the water to collect his prizes without disconnecting the power. At least he never had to pay the electric bill.

Little Johnny is out fishing with his grandfather. They're sitting by the river, waiting and waiting for the fish to bite. Finally, to break up the boredom, little Johnny's grandfather decides to teach his grandson a lesson. He takes out a flask of whiskey from his hip pocket and pours it into a glass. Then he reaches for the bait, pulls out a couple of worms and puts them in the glass full of liquor. The worms become lifeless almost immediately. "Look here, Johnny," his grandfather says. "See that? Those worms have died. What does that tell you, son?"

"Simple, Grandpa," little Johnny answers. "Drink whiskey and you won't get worms."

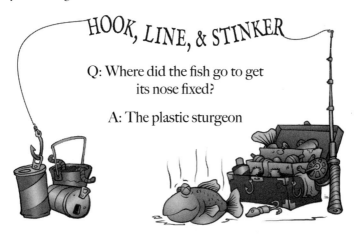

HOOK, LINE, & STINKER

Q: Where did the fish go to get its nose fixed?

A: The plastic sturgeon

Quote, Unquote

Complete the following quote by filling in the missing word.
Its correlating letters can be obtained from the punch lines to the
groaners listed below.

> "I like fishing, but I don't have any patience.
> So I use an _ _ _ _ _ _ _ _." -Craig Sharf

1. Q: What kind of sea creature eats its victims two by two?
   A: Noah's _ _ <u>1</u> <u>5</u> _

2. Q: What do you call a young, neurotic octopus?
   A: A crazy, mixed up _ <u>2</u> <u>3</u> <u>6</u> _

3. Q: Name a musical fish.
   A: _ <u>7</u> _ <u>4</u>

4. Q: Why did the lobster blush?
   A: It saw the Queen Mary's _ _ _ _ _ <u>8</u>.

___ ___ ___ ___ ___ ___ ___ ___
 1   2   3   4   5   6   7   8

Answers
1. Shark
2. Squid
3. Tuna
4. Bottom

> "I like fishing, but I don't have any patience.
> So I use an **aquarium**."

Way down south among the magnolia trees and drooping Spanish moss, there was a muddy old fishing hole that seemed almost as if Huck Finn should be lolling back on the grassy banks, passing the sultry summer afternoons dangling a bent pin in the water and spinning yarns.

Little Johnny and his dog Rex were regular visitors to this idyllic spot, and one day while Johnny was fishing, Rex made a wild leap for a bird and landed in the dark, murky water. Finding it cool and refreshing, Rex was not anxious to come out. When he eventually did, he carried the powerful stench of pond scum and bottom mud.

Little Johnny took his reeking Rex home and tied him to a tree far away from the house so he could go to the store for something to clean the smell off of him.

At the store, Johnny picked up the biggest box of industrial strength laundry detergent that he could find and headed to the checkout.

The shopkeeper, kindly old Mr. Withers, asked little Johnny what the detergent was for, and Johnny told him the story about Rex and the dog's need for a good lathering.

Mr. Withers looked concerned and said, "Johnny, that's some pretty potent stuff there. I don't think it would be good to wash your dog with that."

Little Johnny thought for a moment and decided to take the box anyway.

A week or so later, Johnny was back at the store and Mr. Withers asked him how it went with Rex. "Not so good," Johnny replied. "Rex died.

"Oh, I'm so sorry Johnny," said Mr. Withers. "I did warn you not to use that detergent on him."

"Oh, it wasn't the soap," said little Johnny.

"What did he die of, then?" asked Mr. Withers.

" Well," little Johnny drawled, "The vet thinks it may have been the spin cycle."

Bathroom Graffiti:
Mrs. Paul's Fish Sticks. Does Yours?

• • •

Q: What do you catch when you go ice fishing?
A: A cold

WHAT IS HALF FISH AND
HALF ZEBRA?

TOP TEN PHRASES
NEVER UTTERED BY ANGLERS

#10. "You know, buddy, those hip boots make your butt look big."

#9. "I don't know if duct tape can fix that."

#8. "C'mon man ... We can watch bass fishing anytime! My favorite redecorating show is on."

#7. "You're crazy, man! My truck can't get through that!"

#6. "Better throw some of that beer overboard- the weight is swamping the boat."

#5. "Hey Charlie - rub some of that tanning lotion onto my back, will ya?"

#4. "Let's get the wives ... Fishing just isn't fun without the ladies along."

#3. "I've been thinking. Those environmentalists and animal rights folks just may have a point."

#2. "Maybe we should give up fishing and take up a real sport like badminton."

And the **#1** Phrase Never Uttered By Anglers ...
"Gee, I've never caught a fish that big!"

A STRIPED BASS

Two Chicago tourists, heading to Florida for vacation, had been tooling down hot, dry and dusty roads for hours when they happened to spot a tranquil little spring-fed pond. Sitting on the bank, a small barefoot boy was fishing.

"Yo, Kid!" called one of the tourists. "Are there any snakes in this pond?"

"No, sir," said the lad.

With that, the two dusty and overheated men stripped down to their undies and dove into the water.

After frolicking for a few minutes, one of the men surfaced near the boy and said, "Say, Son, I was just wondering. How do you know for sure there aren't any snakes in this water?"

"Easy," the boy smiled. "The gators ate 'em all."

Q: What do you call the dumbest fish in the school?
A: Dinner

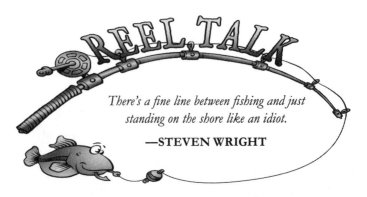

There's a fine line between fishing and just standing on the shore like an idiot.

—STEVEN WRIGHT

Rod & Rhyme

Early to bed
Early to rise
Fish all day
Make up lies.

•

A three-pound pull, and a five-pound bite;
An eight-pound jump, and a ten-pound fight;
A twelve-pound bend to your pole—but alas!
When you get him aboard he's a half-pound bass!

•

An answer to this question
Is what I greatly wish;
Does fishing make men liars—
Or do only liars fish?

•

Old Noah went a-fishing;
He sat upon the ark
And kept his hooks a-dangle
From daybreak on to dark.
His catch was pretty meager,
But everyone affirms
He had not a chance, because he
Had just a pair of worms.

—St. Clair Adams

BUMPER SNICKERS

FISHERMEN GET THE BLUES

• • •

WOMEN WANT ME, FISH FEAR ME

• • •

WHEN FISHERMEN DRINK,
THEY ASSIGN A DESIGNATED DIVER

• • •

FISH STORIES TOLD HERE

• • •

GET REEL!

• • •

I FISH, THEREFORE I LIE

• • •

I CATCH FISH BY THE TALE

• • •

OLD FISHERMEN NEVER DIE,
THEY JUST LOSE THEIR MUSSELS

The Hookie Hook

There's an old joke about a priest playing golf on Sunday instead of being at church. St. Peter, looking down from heaven, asks God just how he's going to punish him. God says, "You'll see." The priest tees off and hits a 350-yard hole-in-one! St. Peter says to God, "You call that punishment?" God answers, "Aha, but who's he going tell?"

In a reel life story, nine-year-old Jarrett Hillman could relate to that. Jarrett and his dad left Beach Haven, New Jersey's Tuna Marlin Club on the morning of June 15, 2011 for some fishing out on the Atlantic Ocean. Some five miles out and 9 hours later, Jarrett felt a tug on his pole. This wasn't your ordinary tug. This was a capital "T"- as in thresher- tug. Jarrett had hooked a thresher shark. A big one. A lot bigger than Jarrett himself. Yet, in a 45-minute tug of war, the 72-pound youngster was able to pull in the 248.5 lb. monster (which measured 75 inches from the nose to the fork in the tail and 70 inches from the tip of the tail to the fork). In the process, Jarrett established an International Game Fishing Association record in the age 10 and under "small fry" division.

But "aha", as God said in the golf groaner, who was Jarrett going to tell? While he was setting a world-class mark, his third grade classmates were sitting in school.

"One brisk morning spent fishing on a misty lake can bring home to a child the beauty, drama and fragility of our natural heritage in a way a thousand classroom presentations never could."
-President George H.W. Bush, in a 1989 message
on the observance of National Fishing Week

DE-FIN-ITIONS

Live bait: the biggest fish you got to handle all day

Thumb: a temporary hook holder

Fisherman: a jerk at one end of the line waiting for a jerk at the other

Sinker: a weight hopefully big enough to knock out any fish on the way to the bottom so that it floats to the surface

Rookie angler: the one who catches the most and biggest fish

Truth: when one fisherman calls another fisherman a liar

• • •

Why does a fish take things in his mouth?
Because he doesn't have any hands.

Fishing, with me, has always been an excuse to drink in the daytime.

—JIMMY CANNON

What do you get if you cross an elephant with a fish?
A pair of swimming trunks

What do you call a man with a fishing pole on his head?
Rod

What do fish use to get in touch with each other?
Shell phones

HOOK, LINE, & STINKER

Q: Why couldn't Batman go fishing?

A: Because Robin ate all the worms

A New York lawyer was fishing at a lake in the backwoods of South Carolina. The bites were few and far between, but the sheer solitude of sitting by the water, relaxing with rod and reel, was a welcome departure from the Big Apple hustle 'n' bustle... or so he thought.

"Hey, you! Get out of here!"

The startled lawyer turned around to see a grizzled old backwoodsman. "This is private property!" yelled the old timer.

"Listen," the lawyer replied. "You may think I'm a city slicker, but I know my way around. This is public property and I can fish here any time I so choose. I'm one of the top litigators in the country and if you give me any more trouble, I'll sue you and take everything you've got. I'll make so much trouble for you that you'll wish you'd never been born."

"Well city boy, if you knew anything at all, you'd know that around here, we don't use courts and judges to settle arguments. We use the Carolina Three Kick Rule."

"What's that?" asked the attorney.

WHAT DO YOU SAY TO A GUY WITH HIS LURE IN THE SEAWEED?

The old woodsman replied, "Well, first I kick you three times, then you kick me three times and we go on like that until somebody gives up."

The lawyer sized the old man up and figured he could take the guy easy.

"Okay, you're on," he said, and with that the woodsman landed his thick boot where it would do the most damage. As the lawyer doubled over and slumped to the ground, he wondered how this old guy managed to kick like a mule.

"Here comes number two," the woodsman barked, just as his boot smashed the lawyer in the teeth, knocking him off his knees and scattering his choppers all over the ground.

The woodsman's last kick came with no warning and impacted the lawyer's head so hard that it spun him over and over until he came to rest right in the muddied waters by the edge of the lake. Severely injured and dazed, the arrogant lawyer struggled to his feet, thirsting for revenge.

"All right, Bubba, you've had you fun," he snarled. "Now it's my turn."

The old geezer shrugged and replied, "Naw – you win. You can fish here."

YOUR FLY'S DOWN!

Fisherman's Prayer

God grant that I may live
to fish until my dying day,
and when the final cast is made
and life has slipped away,
I pray that God's great landing net
will catch me in its sweep,
and in His mercy, God will judge me
big enough to keep.

FISHING LINES

"Fishermen don't lie. They just tell beautiful stories."
-Syngman Rhee

— • —

*"George Washington couldn't have been a fisherman.
He never told a lie."*
-Jeff Kaye

— • —

*"How far a fisherman stretches the truth
depends on the length of his arms."*
-Genevieve Johnson

— • —

"Your typical fisherman is long on optimism and short on memory."
-Ken Polish

— • —

*"Fishing is not a matter of life and death.
It is much more important than that."*
-Jim Tomlinson

"Bragging may not bring happiness, but no man having caught a large fish goes home through an alley."
-Carmine Rende

— • —

"Every man in his life has a fish that haunts him."
-Negley Farson

— • —

"'Angling' is the name given to fishing by people who can't fish."
-Stephen Leacock

— • —

"That sage, Mr. Edward Zern, claimed that 'roughly two-thirds of all fishermen never eat fish.' This should surprise nobody. Fish is brain food. People who eat fish have large, well-developed brains. People with large, well-developed brains don't fish."
-Nick Lyons

— • —

"A fish story backed by visual evidence is something you don't run into every day."
-Red Smith

"Fishing seems to be the favorite form of loafing."
-Ed Howe

— • —

"The fishing was so bad that even the liars didn't catch any."
-Sanford Mims

— • —

"A man has to believe in something. I believe I'll go fishing."
-A.O. Hil

— • —

*"It really is true that when some fishermen
tell a tale, they will go to any length."*
-Tom Tucci

— • —

*"We're fishing and my wife had a problem with killing the fish. I wasn't
crazy with that part either, but I figured if we just wait for them to die
naturally, it could take forever. Certainly 'til after supper."*
-Paul Reiser

— • —

"Fish may be bought if they can't be caught."
-Gene Demers

"I get all the truth I need in the newspaper every morning, and every chance I get I go fishing, or swap stories with fishermen, to get the taste of it out of my mouth."
-Ed Zern

— • —

"Why is it that fish always seem to go on vacation at the same time we do?"
-Bob Matistic

— • —

"A fish wouldn't get caught if it kept its mouth shut."
-Fisherman's saying

— • —

"Suckers are trash fish, an insult to divinity. They have chubby, humanoid lips and appear to be begging for cigars."
-Bill Barich

— • —

"I don't want to sit at the head table anymore. I want to go fishing."
-President George H.W. Bush

— • —

"So frequent the casts. So seldom a strike."
-Arnold Gingrich

"Somebody just back of you while you are fishing is as bad as someone looking over your shoulder while you write a letter to your girl."
-Ernest Hemingway

— • —

"Nothing grows faster than a fish between the time the fish takes the bait...and the time he gets away."
-Tom Lehmann

— • —

"So frequent the casts. So seldom a strike."
-Arnold Gingrich

— • —

"At the altar, I little realized I was pledged to love, honor, and obey three outboard motors, the ways of the river, the whims of the tide, and the wiles of the fish, as well as Bill, the man of my choice."
-Beatrice Cook

— • —

"Scholars have long known that fishing eventually turns men into philosophers. Unfortunately, it is almost impossible to buy decent tackle on a philosopher's salary."
-Patrick F. McManus

"A fish probably goes home and lies about the bait he stole."
-Harry Roy

— • —

"There's nothing a fisherman can do if his worm ain't trying!"
-Sanford Mims

— • —

*"Fishing is the only sport where sitting on your butt
under a tree looks like concentrated activity."*
-Jeff MacNelly

— • —

*"I used to go fishing until it struck me...You can buy fish.
What the hell am I doing in a boat at four-thirty in the morning?
If I want a hamburger, I don't track cattle down."*
-Kenny Potchenson

— • —

*"If anglers talked only about the fish they really caught,
the silence would be unbearable."*
-Dan D'Aloia

— • —

"If a man fishes hard, what is he going to do easy?"
-Roy Blount, Jr.

"You can always tell a fisherman, but you can't tell him much."
-Corey Ford

— • —

"If fishing is like religion, then fly fishing is high church."
-Tom Brokaw

— • —

"Now comes April when intelligent worms go underground because, with the trout season approaching, there is danger of being plucked away from home and loved ones, skewered on a hook and flung into the bitter numbing cold of a mountain brook. This is bad for worms."
-Red Smith

— • —

"It's a crime to catch a fish in some waters, and a miracle in others."
-Geoff Scowcroft

— • —

"In seeing some of the new fishermen on the old riffles, I'm reminded of a friend who told me he's recently taken up golf because he likes the clothes."
-John Merwin

"I watched a fishing show today on television. Have you ever watched fishing for about fifteen minutes and said, 'Boy, I need a life'?"
-Brian Regan

— • —

"Since three-fourths of the earth's surface is water and one-fourth land, it's perfectly clear the good Lord intended that man spend three times as much time fishing as he does plowing."
-Matt Taets

— • —

"When four fishermen get together, there's always a fifth."
-Spencer Apollonio

— • —

"An angler is a man who spends rainy days on the muddy banks of rivers doing nothing because his wife won't let him do it at home."
-Don Champion

— • —

"Man can learn a lot from fishing. When the fish are biting, no problem in the world is big enough to be remembered."
-OA Battista